NIGHT BECOMES DAY

CHANGES IN NATURE

CYNTHIA ARGENTINE

M MILLBROOK PRESS / MINNEAPOLIS

FOR MARK—IT IS A JOY
TO WALK THROUGH LIFE'S
CHANGES WITH YOU. —C.A.

Thank you to Tyler H. Doane, Ph.D., Post-doctoral Fellow, Department of
Earth and Atmospheric Sciences, Indiana University, and Michael P. Eddy, Ph.D.,
Assistant Professor, Department of Earth, Atmospheric, and Planetary Sciences,
Purdue University, for reviewing the text for accuracy and sharing their expertise.

Millbrook Press™
An imprint of Lerner Publishing Group, Inc.
241 First Avenue North
Minneapolis, MN 55401 USA

For reading levels and more information, look up this title at www.lernerbooks.com.

Image credits: Stephanie Starr/EyeEm/Getty Images, pp. 2-3; Kaping Mayo/EyeEm/Getty Images, p. 4 (left);
Chatsushutter/Shutterstock.com, p. 4 (right); Aniko Hobely/Getty Images, p. 5; Aleksandr Ozerov/Shutterstock.com,
p. 6; Amanda Mohler/Shutterstock.com, pp. 6-7, 30; AjayTvm/Shutterstock.com, pp. 8-9; RoboFly/Shutterstock.com,
p. 10 (left); Luxx Images/Getty Images, pp. 10 (right), 31; Justin Wheeler/Getty Images, p. 11; Valdelicio Silva/
Shutterstock.com, p. 12; Ron and Patty Thomas/Getty Images, pp. 12-13, 31; o-lush/Shutterstock.com, pp. 14-15; Sky
Cloud Pics/Shutterstock.com, pp. 16-17; trabantos/Getty Images, pp. 17, 31; Deni_Sugandi/Shutterstock.com, pp. 18-19,
32; Sergejus Lamanosovas/Shutterstock.com, pp. 20-21; Bjoern Wylezich/Shutterstock.com, p. 22; Mariia Tagirova/
Shutterstock.com, pp. 22-23, 32; Matt Gibson/Shutterstock.com, p. 24; Martin Ruegner/Getty Images, pp. 24-25; Kristine Rad/
Shutterstock.com, p. 26 (left); Kamrad71/Shutterstock.com, p. 26 (right); MVolodymyr/Shutterstock.com, p. 27; Vicki Smith/
Getty Images, p. 28; NOPPHARAT7824/Shutterstock.com, p. 29.
Jacket images: Pavel_Klimenko/Shutterstock.com; Kaping Mayo/EyeEm/Getty Images; NOPPHARAT7824/Shutterstock.com;
Aniko Hobely/Getty Images.

Designed by Mary Ross.
Main body text set in Mikado. Typeface provided by HVD Fonts.

Library of Congress Cataloging-in-Publication Data

Names: Argentine, Cynthia, 1966- author.
Title: Night becomes day : changes in nature / Cynthia Argentine.
Description: Minneapolis, MN : Millbrook Press, [2022] | Includes bibliographical references. | Audience: Ages 4-9 | Audience: Grades 2-3 |
    Summary: "Change can be colorful—like leaves in fall. Change can be slow—like a river carving a canyon. Lyrical language and stunning
    photographs explore the transformative power of nature's processes all around us" —Provided by publisher.
Identifiers: LCCN 2021013585 (print) | LCCN 2021013586 (ebook) | ISBN 9781541581241 (library binding) | ISBN 9781728419053 (ebook)
Subjects: LCSH: Nature—Juvenile literature.
Classification: LCC QH48 .A59 2022 (print) | LCC QH48 (ebook) | DDC 508—dc23

LC record available at https://lccn.loc.gov/2021013585
LC ebook record available at https://lccn.loc.gov/2021013586

Manufactured in the United States of America
1-47323-47950-5/5/2021

NIGHT BECOMES DAY.

FLOWER BECOMES FRUIT.

Nature is always at work,

TRANSFORMING.

Some changes are

SMALL,

like footprints
disappearing in sand.

SWOOSH!

The wave retreats.

They're gone . . .

Other changes are 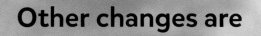**BIG** like a giant canyon.

The river wears away stone, bit by bit, layer by layer.

It carves a canyon thousands of steps deep and hundreds of miles long.

Change can be **QUICK**.
A pumpkin tendril wraps around a rope in minutes.

But often, change is

SLOW.

An acorn lies still on the ground. In a few weeks, it cracks open and sends down a root.

In a few more weeks, it drops its shell, sprouts, and becomes a sapling.

The little oak tree grows,
adding leaves and limbs.

In many years it will offer
shade, shelter, and a perfect
place to climb or rest.

Change can

BRIGHTEN,

splashing the landscape with color.
A desert bursts into bloom after rain.

Or change can

DULL,

making colorful things drab.

On the forest floor, golden leaves
turn into dark brown loam.

Rain falls. Animals scamper.
Worms burrow. Microbes munch.

Lost leaves and fallen branches, now soft underfoot, become soil that will support new life.

Change happens

ABOVE.

Fluffy clouds dot the sky as
warm air rises and cools up high.

And change happens

BELOW.

Water moves through rocks and soil, seeps into an underground cavern, and drips, creating eerie teeth and towers. Unhurried in their dark lair, these mineral spires may grow an inch a century.

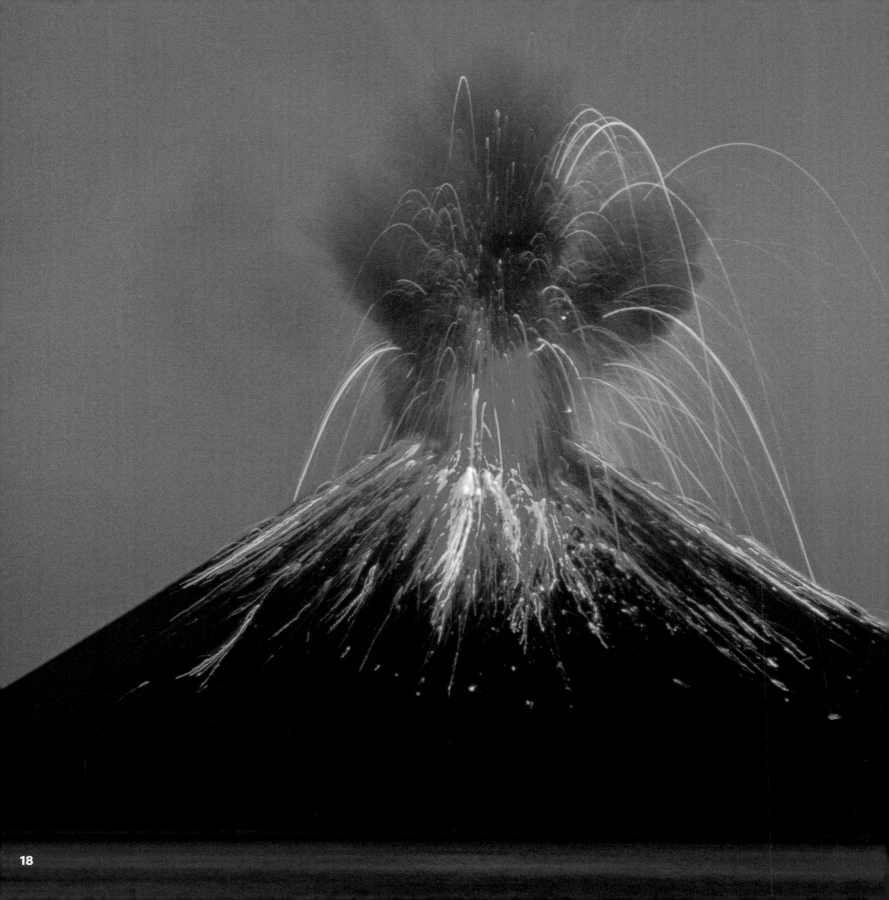

Change can be **HOT**, like a volcano.

Whir, hiss,

rumble, crackle,

KA-BOOM!

Magma bursts from within Earth! Lava glows and flows.

Or change can be **COLD**, like a glacier.

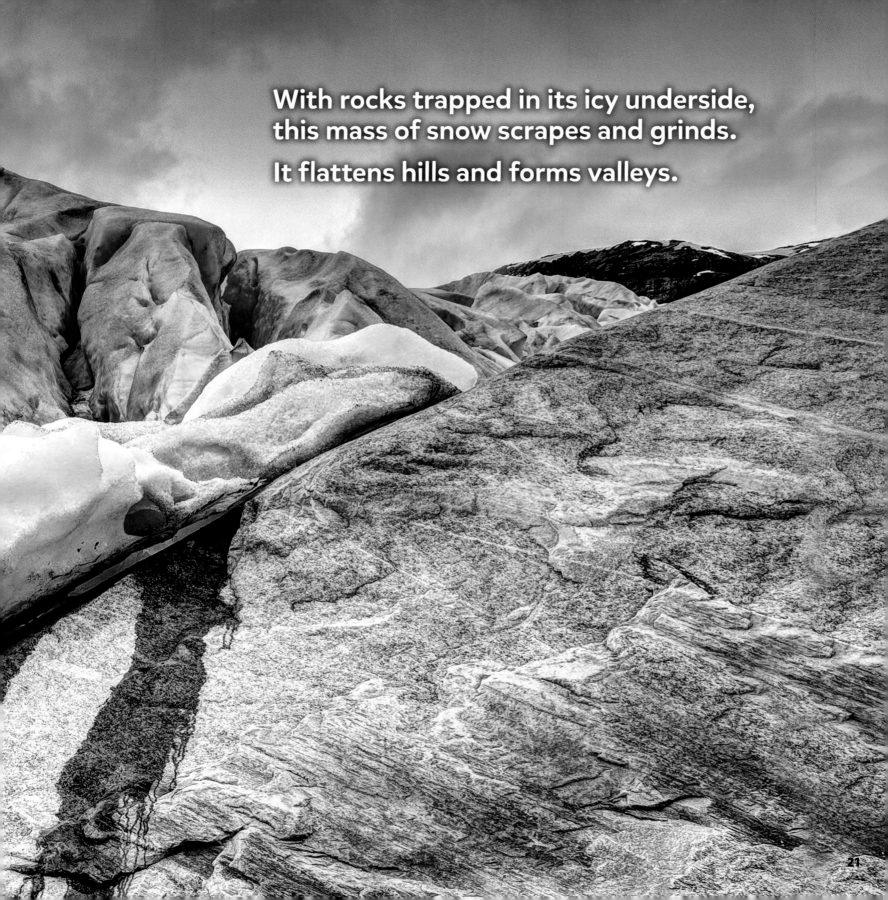

With rocks trapped in its icy underside, this mass of snow scrapes and grinds.

It flattens hills and forms valleys.

Change can be

ANCIENT,

like diamonds. These gems formed eons ago, under intense pressure, deep inside Earth.

But change can also be

NEW, like a snowflake.

A fleck of airborne dust joins a bit of water in the sky to create an ice crystal.

Drifting down, it grows branches and becomes a sparkling star.

Everywhere on Earth—

from shore to mountain,
field to forest, surface to sky—
nature is at work,

TRANSFORMING.

FRUIT
BECOMES
FLOWER.

DAY BECOMES NIGHT.

What

WONDERS

will tomorrow bring?

AUTHOR'S NOTE: CHANGE IN AND AROUND YOU

When you think of changes in nature, what do you think of?

Some changes are so common that people get used to them. We expect seeds to sprout. We expect grass to grow. We expect leaves to change color in the fall. But expected changes can still amaze us. Flowers bloom from bare buds. Birds hatch from quiet eggs. Butterflies emerge from chrysalises and spread new wings. Even within our own bodies, we see changes. Hair grows. Scrapes heal. Our clothes and shoes no longer fit. No one ever stays exactly the same!

Even things that are not alive are always in the process of changing. Think about these examples—waves moving sand, rivers carving canyons, and cave water becoming spires of rock.

Have you ever stopped to think about how living things and nonliving things are connected? The changes that happen to one thing influence others. When temperatures drop and snow falls, animals burrow and hibernate. When a seed sprouts in cracked rock, its roots slowly break the rock apart and allow soil to form there. When sea creatures shed their shells, waves tumble the shells around and mix them with beach sand, where new sea creatures will live and grow.

In one way or another, everything on Earth is connected. The science behind these connections is called *ecology*. When you are outside, or looking out a window, notice things that are changing around you. What do you see? Can you describe how living and nonliving changes might be related?

A CLOSER LOOK AT THE SCIENCE OF CHANGE

BEACHES AND CANYONS

Geology: Changes Involving Land and Water (Pages 6–7)

Bodies of water are powerful agents of change. Oceans are constantly erasing footprints—and sandcastles! They are also reshaping coastlines around the world. Each wave that splashes ashore stirs up sand from the beach and carries it along. When the water slows, the sand settles and arrives in a new location. As a result, the beach moves. Sometimes this action makes whole islands move.

Barrier islands—beach-covered islands close to shorelines—can travel as much as 60 feet (18 m) or more a year.

Rivers also alter the landscape. When rivers and the sediments they carry flow through rocky shores, they carve canyons by beating against the rock and dissolving minerals. When they flow through muddy banks, they cut curves in them. Fast-flowing currents dig away at the outside of bends, and slower currents allow soil to settle, forming new land.

PUMPKIN TENDRILS AND OAK TREES
Botany: Changes Involving Plants (Pages 8–11)

Have you ever seen a plant move itself, right in front of your eyes? Most plants stay put and grow very slowly. But a few plants will move while you watch. If you wait patiently for half an hour, for example, you might be able to watch a tendril of a pumpkin vine curl around your finger.

More often, we think of plants growing and changing quite slowly. An oak tree is a good example. Like many plants, its life is a cycle of change. An acorn sprouts, becomes a sapling, and then a larger tree. The mature tree makes new acorns. This is called a cycle because the pattern repeats.

Some plants sprout, grow, and die in just a few weeks. Others, like oaks, may live for hundreds of years. The oldest trees in the world have lived thousands of years and are older than the United States.

DESERTS AND FORESTS
Biology: Changes Involving Soil (Pages 12–15)

In sun and shade, plants, animals, soil, and water interact to cause change. When rain falls after a long, dry season in a desert, wildflowers sometimes sprout and bloom, carpeting barren land with yellow, blue, pink, and purple blossoms. The desert soil secretly harbors millions of sleeping seeds and microbes. They lie dormant until the right conditions of water, light, and temperature prompt them to wake up and grow.

Deep in a shady forest, dampened by rain, trampled by animals, old leaves and fallen branches transform into dark brown humus. Worms, fungi, and microbes eat and break down the dead plant material. One teaspoon of soil may contain a *billion* microbes. The decomposed matter becomes part of the soil and provides nutrients to new plants, thereby continuing the cycle of life.

CLOUDS AND CAVERNS
Chemistry and Geology: Changes Involving Water, Air, or Minerals (Pages 16–17)

Even when water is not part of an ocean or river, it is involved in change. Water is present in the air around us, but often we can't see it. Sometimes, as pockets of warm, moist air float high in the sky, they expand and cool. Then water molecules come together, attaching to specks of dust and forming tiny droplets. Suspended in the air, these droplets—much smaller than raindrops—form clouds. This is similar to what happens on cool mornings when dew appears. Water molecules in the air condense, or draw together, and form sparkling spheres on blades of grass.

Water is also underground, flowing through openings within soil and rock. The water entering caves slowly dissolves minerals in the rock walls. The minerals disappear like sugar in tea. When the water drips, minerals travel with it. As gas escapes from the drip water, minerals are left behind. These minerals recrystallize and create new rocks. The ones that look like teeth hanging from the ceiling are stalactites. The ones growing up from the ground are stalagmites.

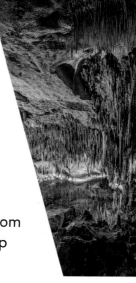

VOLCANOES AND GLACIERS
Geology: Changes Involving Sheets of Land or Ice (Pages 18–21)

Hot volcanoes and cold glaciers powerfully affect the shape of the land around them. Volcanoes are like vents. They allow hot steam and molten rock to escape from inside Earth. Many volcanoes are in mountain ranges near oceans. They form when the tectonic plate (a huge sheet of rock) below the ocean slides beneath the tectonic plate below the adjacent land. This causes magma, or hot, melted rock, to form deep within Earth and to rise to the surface. When the pressure inside that molten rock gets high enough, it explodes. Hot rock, gases, and ash burst into the air from volcanoes.

Glaciers, or huge sheets of ice, are like giant scraping tools. In high altitudes or other cold regions, snow falls each year and collects between hills or mountains. It packs down under its own weight to form a glacier. Pulled by gravity, glaciers slowly slide downhill. As they move, the rocks caught within them carve away land, creating deep valleys and other landforms.

DIAMONDS AND SNOWFLAKES
Chemistry, Geology, and Physics: Changes Involving Crystals (Pages 22–23)

Diamonds and snowflakes are both clear crystals. One is very strong, and the other is very fragile. Diamonds are one of the hardest substances on Earth. They are composed of carbon, the same element that—in different forms—makes up the graphite in pencils and is a component of all living things.

Most diamonds used in jewelry formed long ago in Earth's mantle miles beneath the surface. This is deeper than machines can drill. The extremely high temperatures and pressures in this part of Earth caused atoms of carbon to fit together so tightly that they formed a diamond crystal structure. Ancient volcanic eruptions shot these diamonds up through pipelike pathways to depths that can be mined.

Diamonds have also been found in craters where asteroids have struck. When an asteroid crashes into Earth, it creates immense pressure and heat, with temperatures possibly reaching thousands of degrees. Scientists believe these extreme forces may transform carbon at the crash site into tiny diamonds.

Snowflakes, however, are so fragile that a breath can make them disappear. They form when water below the freezing point (around 32°F, or 0°C) latches onto specks of dust high in the air. From these tiny "seeds," snowflake crystals begin to grow. More water molecules attach and arrange themselves, becoming the six-sided, symmetric shapes we call snowflakes.